Income & Expenses Log Book for Teenagers

Published by Jenny Little
Copyright © 2018 Jenny Little

ISBN: 9781983280689

How to use this book

This **Income & Expenses Log Book** is to help you begin to learn more about your spending habits and the importance of having savings.

When you first start to earn your own money (be it pocket money or a part-time job) it can be tempting to go out and spend all of your earnings in one go! It might be fun and what your friends seem to be doing but creating a habit of saving money and learning how to budget will be really useful to you when it comes to buying more expensive items as you grow older.

Buying a car, going to college, paying rent – the list goes on! If you already have some savings you will find it much easier and if you know how to keep a check on your income and expenses, you'll be less likely to end up with a huge debt that you struggle to pay off.

This book has weekly income and expenses tables for you to fill in and then a summary section for the week. This will enable you to see at a glance how much money you are left with and then you can decide what you want to do with it.

For example, are there birthday presents you need to buy or some other expense that you know of? Perhaps you are saving up for something special and want to put some money aside for that? Is there any money left over that you could put into a savings account – even a small amount put away each week will add up over time.

Fill in the '*Weekly Summary*' and '*What will I do with my money*' sections each week to stay up to date with future expenses that you need to keep money available for and any potential savings you can deposit.

Don't forget to brainstorm ideas of things you really want for yourself and are prepared to save up for. When you have enough money to buy any of those things, you can tick them off the list and enjoy the feeling of satisfaction that comes from saving up and buying something all by yourself.

Weekly Income				
Date	No. of Hours	Employer & Description	Via Cash /Bank?	Amount Paid
			Total Income	

Weekly Summary

Total Income	
Total Expenses	
Total (income minus expenses)	

Specific Things I'm Saving Up For

Item Description	How Much it Costs	Have I Got it Yet?
		☐
		☐
		☐
		☐

Weekly Expenses

Date	Item(s) Bought	Purchased Where?	Via Cash /Bank?	Cost
		Total Expenses		

What will I do with my money?

Can I put some money into a Savings Account?	Existing Balance	Amount Deposited	New Savings Balance

Any expenses coming up that I need to remember? (e.g. birthdays, holidays)	

Can I afford what I'm saving up for?	

Money Left Over This Week	

(This is the **Total** from your **Weekly Summary**, minus the **Amount Deposited** into your Savings Account)

Weekly Income

Date	No. of Hours	Employer & Description	Via Cash /Bank?	Amount Paid
			Total Income	

Weekly Summary

Total Income	
Total Expenses	
Total	
Money Left Over from Last Week	
Total Amount Left (Total + Money Left from Last Week)	

Specific Things I'm Saving Up For

Item Description	How Much it Costs	Have I Got it Yet?
		☐
		☐
		☐
		☐

Weekly Expenses

Date	Item(s) Bought	Purchased Where?	Via Cash /Bank?	Cost
		Total Expenses		

What will I do with my money?

Can I put some money into a Savings Account?	Existing Balance	Amount Deposited	New Savings Balance

Any expenses coming up that I need to remember? (e.g. birthdays, holidays)	

Can I afford what I'm saving up for?	

Money Left Over This Week	

(This is the **Total Amount Left** from your **Weekly Summary**, minus the **Amount Deposited** into your Savings Account)

Weekly Income

Date	No. of Hours	Employer & Description	Via Cash /Bank?	Amount Paid
			Total Income	

Weekly Summary

Total Income	
Total Expenses	
Total	
Money Left Over from Last Week	
Total Amount Left	

Specific Things I'm Saving Up For

Item Description	How Much it Costs	Have I Got it Yet?
		☐
		☐
		☐
		☐

Weekly Expenses				
Date	Item(s) Bought	Purchased Where?	Via Cash /Bank?	Cost
			Total Expenses	

What will I do with my money?

Can I put some money into a Savings Account?	Existing Balance	Amount Deposited	New Savings Balance

Any expenses coming up that I need to remember? (e.g. birthdays, holidays)	

Can I afford what I'm saving up for?	

Money Left Over This Week	

(This is the **Total Amount Left** from your **Weekly Summary**, minus the **Amount Deposited** into your Savings Account)

Weekly Income

Date	No. of Hours	Employer & Description	Via Cash /Bank?	Amount Paid
			Total Income	

Weekly Summary

Total Income	
Total Expenses	
Total	
Money Left Over from Last Week	
Total Amount Left	

Specific Things I'm Saving Up For

Item Description	How Much it Costs	Have I Got it Yet?
		☐
		☐
		☐
		☐

Weekly Expenses

Date	Item(s) Bought	Purchased Where?	Via Cash /Bank?	Cost
			Total Expenses	

What will I do with my money?

Can I put some money into a Savings Account?	Existing Balance	Amount Deposited	New Savings Balance

Any expenses coming up that I need to remember? (e.g. birthdays, holidays)	

Can I afford what I'm saving up for?	

Money Left Over This Week	

(This is the **Total Amount Left** from your **Weekly Summary**, minus the **Amount Deposited** into your Savings Account)

Weekly Income				
Date	No. of Hours	Employer & Description	Via Cash /Bank?	Amount Paid
			Total Income	

Weekly Summary

Total Income	
Total Expenses	
Total	
Money Left Over from Last Week	
Total Amount Left	

Specific Things I'm Saving Up For

Item Description	How Much it Costs	Have I Got it Yet?
		☐
		☐
		☐
		☐

Weekly Expenses

Date	Item(s) Bought	Purchased Where?	Via Cash /Bank?	Cost
		Total Expenses		

What will I do with my money?

Can I put some money into a Savings Account?	Existing Balance	Amount Deposited	New Savings Balance

Any expenses coming up that I need to remember? (e.g. birthdays, holidays)	

Can I afford what I'm saving up for?	

Money Left Over This Week	

(This is the **Total Amount Left** from your **Weekly Summary**, minus the **Amount Deposited** into your Savings Account)

Weekly Income				
Date	No. of Hours	Employer & Description	Via Cash /Bank?	Amount Paid
			Total Income	

Weekly Summary

Total Income	
Total Expenses	
Total	
Money Left Over from Last Week	
Total Amount Left	

Specific Things I'm Saving Up For

Item Description	How Much it Costs	Have I Got it Yet?
		☐
		☐
		☐
		☐

Weekly Expenses

Date	Item(s) Bought	Purchased Where?	Via Cash /Bank?	Cost
			Total Expenses	

What will I do with my money?

Can I put some money into a Savings Account?	Existing Balance	Amount Deposited	New Savings Balance

Any expenses coming up that I need to remember? (e.g. birthdays, holidays)	

Can I afford what I'm saving up for?	

Money Left Over This Week	

(This is the **Total Amount Left** from your **Weekly Summary**, minus the **Amount Deposited** into your Savings Account)

Weekly Income				
Date	No. of Hours	Employer & Description	Via Cash /Bank?	Amount Paid
			Total Income	

Weekly Summary

Total Income	
Total Expenses	
Total	
Money Left Over from Last Week	
Total Amount Left	

Specific Things I'm Saving Up For

Item Description	How Much it Costs	Have I Got it Yet?
		☐
		☐
		☐
		☐

Weekly Expenses				
Date	Item(s) Bought	Purchased Where?	Via Cash /Bank?	Cost
			Total Expenses	

What will I do with my money?

Can I put some money into a Savings Account?	Existing Balance	Amount Deposited	New Savings Balance

Any expenses coming up that I need to remember? (e.g. birthdays, holidays)	

Can I afford what I'm saving up for?	

Money Left Over This Week	

(This is the **Total Amount Left** from your **Weekly Summary**, minus the **Amount Deposited** into your Savings Account)

Weekly Income				
Date	No. of Hours	Employer & Description	Via Cash /Bank?	Amount Paid
			Total Income	

Weekly Summary

Total Income	
Total Expenses	
Total	
Money Left Over from Last Week	
Total Amount Left	

Specific Things I'm Saving Up For

Item Description	How Much it Costs	Have I Got it Yet?
		☐
		☐
		☐
		☐

Weekly Expenses				
Date	Item(s) Bought	Purchased Where?	Via Cash /Bank?	Cost
			Total Expenses	

What will I do with my money?

Can I put some money into a Savings Account?	Existing Balance	Amount Deposited	New Savings Balance

Any expenses coming up that I need to remember? (e.g. birthdays, holidays)	

Can I afford what I'm saving up for?	

Money Left Over This Week	

(This is the **Total Amount Left** from your **Weekly Summary**, minus the
Amount Deposited into your Savings Account)

Weekly Income				
Date	No. of Hours	Employer & Description	Via Cash /Bank?	Amount Paid
			Total Income	

Weekly Summary

Total Income	
Total Expenses	
Total	
Money Left Over from Last Week	
Total Amount Left	

Specific Things I'm Saving Up For

Item Description	How Much it Costs	Have I Got it Yet?
		☐
		☐
		☐
		☐

Weekly Expenses

Date	Item(s) Bought	Purchased Where?	Via Cash /Bank?	Cost
			Total Expenses	

What will I do with my money?

Can I put some money into a Savings Account?	Existing Balance	Amount Deposited	New Savings Balance

Any expenses coming up that I need to remember? (e.g. birthdays, holidays)	

Can I afford what I'm saving up for?	

Money Left Over This Week	

(This is the **Total Amount Left** from your **Weekly Summary**, minus the **Amount Deposited** into your Savings Account)

Weekly Income				
Date	No. of Hours	Employer & Description	Via Cash /Bank?	Amount Paid
			Total Income	

Weekly Summary

Total Income	
Total Expenses	
Total	
Money Left Over from Last Week	
Total Amount Left	

Specific Things I'm Saving Up For

Item Description	How Much it Costs	Have I Got it Yet?
		☐
		☐
		☐
		☐

Weekly Expenses

Date	Item(s) Bought	Purchased Where?	Via Cash /Bank?	Cost
			Total Expenses	

What will I do with my money?

Can I put some money into a Savings Account?	Existing Balance	Amount Deposited	New Savings Balance

Any expenses coming up that I need to remember? (e.g. birthdays, holidays)	

Can I afford what I'm saving up for?	

Money Left Over This Week	

(This is the **Total Amount Left** from your **Weekly Summary**, minus the **Amount Deposited** into your Savings Account)

Weekly Income

Date	No. of Hours	Employer & Description	Via Cash /Bank?	Amount Paid
			Total Income	

Weekly Summary

Total Income	
Total Expenses	
Total	
Money Left Over from Last Week	
Total Amount Left	

Specific Things I'm Saving Up For

Item Description	How Much it Costs	Have I Got it Yet?
		☐
		☐
		☐
		☐

Weekly Expenses

Date	Item(s) Bought	Purchased Where?	Via Cash /Bank?	Cost
		Total Expenses		

What will I do with my money?

Can I put some money into a Savings Account?	Existing Balance	Amount Deposited	New Savings Balance

Any expenses coming up that I need to remember? (e.g. birthdays, holidays)	

Can I afford what I'm saving up for?	

Money Left Over This Week	

(This is the **Total Amount Left** from your **Weekly Summary**, minus the **Amount Deposited** into your Savings Account)

Weekly Income

Date	No. of Hours	Employer & Description	Via Cash /Bank?	Amount Paid
			Total Income	

Weekly Summary

Total Income	
Total Expenses	
Total	
Money Left Over from Last Week	
Total Amount Left	

Specific Things I'm Saving Up For

Item Description	How Much it Costs	Have I Got it Yet?
		☐
		☐
		☐
		☐

Weekly Expenses

Date	Item(s) Bought	Purchased Where?	Via Cash /Bank?	Cost
			Total Expenses	

What will I do with my money?

Can I put some money into a Savings Account?	Existing Balance	Amount Deposited	New Savings Balance

Any expenses coming up that I need to remember? (e.g. birthdays, holidays)	

Can I afford what I'm saving up for?	

Money Left Over This Week	

(This is the **Total Amount Left** from your **Weekly Summary**, minus the **Amount Deposited** into your Savings Account)

Weekly Income

Date	No. of Hours	Employer & Description	Via Cash /Bank?	Amount Paid
			Total Income	

Weekly Summary

Total Income	
Total Expenses	
Total	
Money Left Over from Last Week	
Total Amount Left	

Specific Things I'm Saving Up For

Item Description	How Much it Costs	Have I Got it Yet?
		☐
		☐
		☐
		☐

Weekly Expenses				
Date	Item(s) Bought	Purchased Where?	Via Cash /Bank?	Cost
			Total Expenses	

What will I do with my money?

Can I put some money into a Savings Account?	Existing Balance	Amount Deposited	New Savings Balance

Any expenses coming up that I need to remember? (e.g. birthdays, holidays)	

Can I afford what I'm saving up for?	

Money Left Over This Week	

(This is the **Total Amount Left** from your **Weekly Summary**, minus the **Amount Deposited** into your Savings Account)

Weekly Income				
Date	No. of Hours	Employer & Description	Via Cash /Bank?	Amount Paid
			Total Income	

Weekly Summary

Total Income	
Total Expenses	
Total	
Money Left Over from Last Week	
Total Amount Left	

Specific Things I'm Saving Up For

Item Description	How Much it Costs	Have I Got it Yet?
		☐
		☐
		☐
		☐

Weekly Expenses				
Date	Item(s) Bought	Purchased Where?	Via Cash /Bank?	Cost
			Total Expenses	

What will I do with my money?

Can I put some money into a Savings Account?	Existing Balance	Amount Deposited	New Savings Balance

Any expenses coming up that I need to remember? (e.g. birthdays, holidays)	

Can I afford what I'm saving up for?	

Money Left Over This Week	

(This is the **Total Amount Left** from your **Weekly Summary**, minus the **Amount Deposited** into your Savings Account)

Weekly Income				
Date	No. of Hours	Employer & Description	Via Cash /Bank?	Amount Paid
			Total Income	

Weekly Summary

Total Income	
Total Expenses	
Total	
Money Left Over from Last Week	
Total Amount Left	

Specific Things I'm Saving Up For

Item Description	How Much it Costs	Have I Got it Yet?
		☐
		☐
		☐
		☐

Weekly Expenses

Date	Item(s) Bought	Purchased Where?	Via Cash /Bank?	Cost
		Total Expenses		

What will I do with my money?

Can I put some money into a Savings Account?	Existing Balance	Amount Deposited	New Savings Balance

Any expenses coming up that I need to remember? (e.g. birthdays, holidays)	

Can I afford what I'm saving up for?	

Money Left Over This Week	

(This is the **Total Amount Left** from your **Weekly Summary**, minus the **Amount Deposited** into your Savings Account)

Weekly Income

Date	No. of Hours	Employer & Description	Via Cash /Bank?	Amount Paid
		Total Income		

Weekly Summary

Total Income	
Total Expenses	
Total	
Money Left Over from Last Week	
Total Amount Left	

Specific Things I'm Saving Up For

Item Description	How Much it Costs	Have I Got it Yet?
		☐
		☐
		☐
		☐

Weekly Expenses

Date	Item(s) Bought	Purchased Where?	Via Cash /Bank?	Cost
		Total Expenses		

What will I do with my money?

Can I put some money into a Savings Account?	Existing Balance	Amount Deposited	New Savings Balance

Any expenses coming up that I need to remember? (e.g. birthdays, holidays)	

Can I afford what I'm saving up for?	

Money Left Over This Week	

(This is the **Total Amount Left** from your **Weekly Summary**, minus the **Amount Deposited** into your Savings Account)

Weekly Income

Date	No. of Hours	Employer & Description	Via Cash /Bank?	Amount Paid
			Total Income	

Weekly Summary

Total Income	
Total Expenses	
Total	
Money Left Over from Last Week	
Total Amount Left	

Specific Things I'm Saving Up For

Item Description	How Much it Costs	Have I Got it Yet?
		☐
		☐
		☐
		☐

Weekly Expenses

Date	Item(s) Bought	Purchased Where?	Via Cash /Bank?	Cost
			Total Expenses	

What will I do with my money?

Can I put some money into a Savings Account?	Existing Balance	Amount Deposited	New Savings Balance

Any expenses coming up that I need to remember? (e.g. birthdays, holidays)	

Can I afford what I'm saving up for?	

Money Left Over This Week	

(This is the **Total Amount Left** from your **Weekly Summary**, minus the **Amount Deposited** into your Savings Account)

Weekly Income

Date	No. of Hours	Employer & Description	Via Cash /Bank?	Amount Paid
		Total Income		

Weekly Summary

Total Income	
Total Expenses	
Total	
Money Left Over from Last Week	
Total Amount Left	

Specific Things I'm Saving Up For

Item Description	How Much it Costs	Have I Got it Yet?
		☐
		☐
		☐
		☐

Weekly Expenses

Date	Item(s) Bought	Purchased Where?	Via Cash /Bank?	Cost
			Total Expenses	

What will I do with my money?

Can I put some money into a Savings Account?	Existing Balance	Amount Deposited	New Savings Balance

Any expenses coming up that I need to remember? (e.g. birthdays, holidays)	

Can I afford what I'm saving up for?	

Money Left Over This Week	

(This is the **Total Amount Left** from your **Weekly Summary**, minus the **Amount Deposited** into your Savings Account)

Weekly Income

Date	No. of Hours	Employer & Description	Via Cash /Bank?	Amount Paid
			Total Income	

Weekly Summary

Total Income	
Total Expenses	
Total	
Money Left Over from Last Week	
Total Amount Left	

Specific Things I'm Saving Up For

Item Description	How Much it Costs	Have I Got it Yet?
		☐
		☐
		☐
		☐

Weekly Expenses

Date	Item(s) Bought	Purchased Where?	Via Cash /Bank?	Cost
			Total Expenses	

What will I do with my money?

Can I put some money into a Savings Account?	Existing Balance	Amount Deposited	New Savings Balance

Any expenses coming up that I need to remember? (e.g. birthdays, holidays)	

Can I afford what I'm saving up for?	

Money Left Over This Week	

(This is the **Total Amount Left** from your **Weekly Summary**, minus the **Amount Deposited** into your Savings Account)

Weekly Income

Date	No. of Hours	Employer & Description	Via Cash /Bank?	Amount Paid
			Total Income	

Weekly Summary

Total Income	
Total Expenses	
Total	
Money Left Over from Last Week	
Total Amount Left	

Specific Things I'm Saving Up For

Item Description	How Much it Costs	Have I Got it Yet?
		☐
		☐
		☐
		☐

Weekly Expenses

Date	Item(s) Bought	Purchased Where?	Via Cash /Bank?	Cost
			Total Expenses	

What will I do with my money?

Can I put some money into a Savings Account?	Existing Balance	Amount Deposited	New Savings Balance

Any expenses coming up that I need to remember? (e.g. birthdays, holidays)	

Can I afford what I'm saving up for?	

Money Left Over This Week	

(This is the **Total Amount Left** from your **Weekly Summary**, minus the **Amount Deposited** into your Savings Account)

Weekly Income				
Date	No. of Hours	Employer & Description	Via Cash /Bank?	Amount Paid
			Total Income	

Weekly Summary

Total Income	
Total Expenses	
Total	
Money Left Over from Last Week	
Total Amount Left	

Specific Things I'm Saving Up For

Item Description	How Much it Costs	Have I Got it Yet?
		☐
		☐
		☐
		☐

Weekly Expenses

Date	Item(s) Bought	Purchased Where?	Via Cash /Bank?	Cost
		Total Expenses		

What will I do with my money?

Can I put some money into a Savings Account?	Existing Balance	Amount Deposited	New Savings Balance

Any expenses coming up that I need to remember? (e.g. birthdays, holidays)	

Can I afford what I'm saving up for?	

Money Left Over This Week	

(This is the **Total Amount Left** from your **Weekly Summary**, minus the **Amount Deposited** into your Savings Account)

Weekly Income				
Date	No. of Hours	Employer & Description	Via Cash /Bank?	Amount Paid
			Total Income	

Weekly Summary

Total Income	
Total Expenses	
Total	
Money Left Over from Last Week	
Total Amount Left	

Specific Things I'm Saving Up For

Item Description	How Much it Costs	Have I Got it Yet?
		☐
		☐
		☐
		☐

Weekly Expenses

Date	Item(s) Bought	Purchased Where?	Via Cash /Bank?	Cost
		Total Expenses		

What will I do with my money?

Can I put some money into a Savings Account?	Existing Balance	Amount Deposited	New Savings Balance

Any expenses coming up that I need to remember? (e.g. birthdays, holidays)	

Can I afford what I'm saving up for?	

Money Left Over This Week	

(This is the **Total Amount Left** from your **Weekly Summary**, minus the **Amount Deposited** into your Savings Account)

Weekly Income				
Date	No. of Hours	Employer & Description	Via Cash /Bank?	Amount Paid
			Total Income	

Weekly Summary

Total Income	
Total Expenses	
Total	
Money Left Over from Last Week	
Total Amount Left	

Specific Things I'm Saving Up For

Item Description	How Much it Costs	Have I Got it Yet?
		☐
		☐
		☐
		☐

Weekly Expenses

Date	Item(s) Bought	Purchased Where?	Via Cash /Bank?	Cost
		Total Expenses		

What will I do with my money?

Can I put some money into a Savings Account?	Existing Balance	Amount Deposited	New Savings Balance

Any expenses coming up that I need to remember? (e.g. birthdays, holidays)	

Can I afford what I'm saving up for?	

Money Left Over This Week	

(This is the **Total Amount Left** from your **Weekly Summary**, minus the **Amount Deposited** into your Savings Account)

Weekly Income

Date	No. of Hours	Employer & Description	Via Cash /Bank?	Amount Paid
			Total Income	

Weekly Summary

Total Income	
Total Expenses	
Total	
Money Left Over from Last Week	
Total Amount Left	

Specific Things I'm Saving Up For

Item Description	How Much it Costs	Have I Got it Yet?
		☐
		☐
		☐
		☐

Weekly Expenses

Date	Item(s) Bought	Purchased Where?	Via Cash /Bank?	Cost
		Total Expenses		

What will I do with my money?

Can I put some money into a Savings Account?	Existing Balance	Amount Deposited	New Savings Balance

Any expenses coming up that I need to remember? (e.g. birthdays, holidays)	

Can I afford what I'm saving up for?	

Money Left Over This Week	

(This is the **Total Amount Left** from your **Weekly Summary**, minus the **Amount Deposited** into your Savings Account)

Weekly Income				
Date	No. of Hours	Employer & Description	Via Cash /Bank?	Amount Paid
			Total Income	

Weekly Summary

Total Income	
Total Expenses	
Total	
Money Left Over from Last Week	
Total Amount Left	

Specific Things I'm Saving Up For

Item Description	How Much it Costs	Have I Got it Yet?
		☐
		☐
		☐
		☐

Weekly Expenses				
Date	Item(s) Bought	Purchased Where?	Via Cash /Bank?	Cost
			Total Expenses	

What will I do with my money?

Can I put some money into a Savings Account?	Existing Balance	Amount Deposited	New Savings Balance

Any expenses coming up that I need to remember? (e.g. birthdays, holidays)	

Can I afford what I'm saving up for?	

Money Left Over This Week	

(This is the **Total Amount Left** from your **Weekly Summary**, minus the **Amount Deposited** into your Savings Account)

Weekly Income				
Date	No. of Hours	Employer & Description	Via Cash /Bank?	Amount Paid
			Total Income	

Weekly Summary

Total Income	
Total Expenses	
Total	
Money Left Over from Last Week	
Total Amount Left	

Specific Things I'm Saving Up For

Item Description	How Much it Costs	Have I Got it Yet?
		☐
		☐
		☐
		☐

Weekly Expenses

Date	Item(s) Bought	Purchased Where?	Via Cash /Bank?	Cost
		Total Expenses		

What will I do with my money?

Can I put some money into a Savings Account?	Existing Balance	Amount Deposited	New Savings Balance

Any expenses coming up that I need to remember? (e.g. birthdays, holidays)	

Can I afford what I'm saving up for?	

Money Left Over This Week	

(This is the **Total Amount Left** from your **Weekly Summary**, minus the **Amount Deposited** into your Savings Account)

Weekly Income				
Date	No. of Hours	Employer & Description	Via Cash /Bank?	Amount Paid
			Total Income	

Weekly Summary

Total Income	
Total Expenses	
Total	
Money Left Over from Last Week	
Total Amount Left	

Specific Things I'm Saving Up For

Item Description	How Much it Costs	Have I Got it Yet?
		☐
		☐
		☐
		☐

Weekly Expenses				
Date	Item(s) Bought	Purchased Where?	Via Cash /Bank?	Cost
			Total Expenses	

What will I do with my money?

Can I put some money into a Savings Account?	Existing Balance	Amount Deposited	New Savings Balance

Any expenses coming up that I need to remember? (e.g. birthdays, holidays)	

Can I afford what I'm saving up for?	

Money Left Over This Week	

(This is the **Total Amount Left** from your **Weekly Summary**, minus the **Amount Deposited** into your Savings Account)

Weekly Income				
Date	No. of Hours	Employer & Description	Via Cash /Bank?	Amount Paid
			Total Income	

Weekly Summary

Total Income	
Total Expenses	
Total	
Money Left Over from Last Week	
Total Amount Left	

Specific Things I'm Saving Up For

Item Description	How Much it Costs	Have I Got it Yet?
		☐
		☐
		☐
		☐

Weekly Expenses

Date	Item(s) Bought	Purchased Where?	Via Cash /Bank?	Cost
			Total Expenses	

What will I do with my money?

Can I put some money into a Savings Account?	Existing Balance	Amount Deposited	New Savings Balance

Any expenses coming up that I need to remember? (e.g. birthdays, holidays)	

Can I afford what I'm saving up for?	

Money Left Over This Week	

(This is the **Total Amount Left** from your **Weekly Summary**, minus the **Amount Deposited** into your Savings Account)

Weekly Income				
Date	No. of Hours	Employer & Description	Via Cash /Bank?	Amount Paid
			Total Income	

Weekly Summary

Total Income	
Total Expenses	
Total	
Money Left Over from Last Week	
Total Amount Left	

Specific Things I'm Saving Up For

Item Description	How Much it Costs	Have I Got it Yet?
		☐
		☐
		☐
		☐

Weekly Expenses				
Date	Item(s) Bought	Purchased Where?	Via Cash /Bank?	Cost
			Total Expenses	

What will I do with my money?

Can I put some money into a Savings Account?	Existing Balance	Amount Deposited	New Savings Balance

Any expenses coming up that I need to remember? (e.g. birthdays, holidays)	

Can I afford what I'm saving up for?	

Money Left Over This Week	

(This is the **Total Amount Left** from your **Weekly Summary**, minus the **Amount Deposited** into your Savings Account)

Weekly Income				
Date	No. of Hours	Employer & Description	Via Cash /Bank?	Amount Paid
			Total Income	

Weekly Summary

Total Income	
Total Expenses	
Total	
Money Left Over from Last Week	
Total Amount Left	

Specific Things I'm Saving Up For

Item Description	How Much it Costs	Have I Got it Yet?
		☐
		☐
		☐
		☐

Weekly Expenses				
Date	Item(s) Bought	Purchased Where?	Via Cash /Bank?	Cost
			Total Expenses	

What will I do with my money?

Can I put some money into a Savings Account?	Existing Balance	Amount Deposited	New Savings Balance

Any expenses coming up that I need to remember? (e.g. birthdays, holidays)	

Can I afford what I'm saving up for?	

Money Left Over This Week	

(This is the **Total Amount Left** from your **Weekly Summary**, minus the **Amount Deposited** into your Savings Account)

Weekly Income

Date	No. of Hours	Employer & Description	Via Cash /Bank?	Amount Paid
			Total Income	

Weekly Summary

Total Income	
Total Expenses	
Total	
Money Left Over from Last Week	
Total Amount Left	

Specific Things I'm Saving Up For

Item Description	How Much it Costs	Have I Got it Yet?
		☐
		☐
		☐
		☐

Weekly Expenses

Date	Item(s) Bought	Purchased Where?	Via Cash /Bank?	Cost
		Total Expenses		

What will I do with my money?

Can I put some money into a Savings Account?	Existing Balance	Amount Deposited	New Savings Balance

Any expenses coming up that I need to remember? (e.g. birthdays, holidays)	

Can I afford what I'm saving up for?	

Money Left Over This Week	

(This is the **Total Amount Left** from your **Weekly Summary**, minus the **Amount Deposited** into your Savings Account)

Weekly Income

Date	No. of Hours	Employer & Description	Via Cash /Bank?	Amount Paid
			Total Income	

Weekly Summary

Total Income	
Total Expenses	
Total	
Money Left Over from Last Week	
Total Amount Left	

Specific Things I'm Saving Up For

Item Description	How Much it Costs	Have I Got it Yet?
		☐
		☐
		☐
		☐

Weekly Expenses				
Date	Item(s) Bought	Purchased Where?	Via Cash /Bank?	Cost
			Total Expenses	

What will I do with my money?

Can I put some money into a Savings Account?	Existing Balance	Amount Deposited	New Savings Balance

Any expenses coming up that I need to remember? (e.g. birthdays, holidays)	

Can I afford what I'm saving up for?	

Money Left Over This Week	

(This is the **Total Amount Left** from your **Weekly Summary**, minus the **Amount Deposited** into your Savings Account)

Weekly Income				
Date	No. of Hours	Employer & Description	Via Cash /Bank?	Amount Paid
			Total Income	

Weekly Summary

Total Income	
Total Expenses	
Total	
Money Left Over from Last Week	
Total Amount Left	

Specific Things I'm Saving Up For

Item Description	How Much it Costs	Have I Got it Yet?
		☐
		☐
		☐
		☐

Weekly Expenses				
Date	Item(s) Bought	Purchased Where?	Via Cash /Bank?	Cost
			Total Expenses	

What will I do with my money?

Can I put some money into a Savings Account?	Existing Balance	Amount Deposited	New Savings Balance

Any expenses coming up that I need to remember? (e.g. birthdays, holidays)	

Can I afford what I'm saving up for?	

Money Left Over This Week	

(This is the **Total Amount Left** from your **Weekly Summary**, minus the **Amount Deposited** into your Savings Account)

Weekly Income				
Date	No. of Hours	Employer & Description	Via Cash /Bank?	Amount Paid
			Total Income	

Weekly Summary

Total Income	
Total Expenses	
Total	
Money Left Over from Last Week	
Total Amount Left	

Specific Things I'm Saving Up For

Item Description	How Much it Costs	Have I Got it Yet?
		☐
		☐
		☐
		☐

Weekly Expenses

Date	Item(s) Bought	Purchased Where?	Via Cash /Bank?	Cost
		Total Expenses		

What will I do with my money?

Can I put some money into a Savings Account?	Existing Balance	Amount Deposited	New Savings Balance

Any expenses coming up that I need to remember? (e.g. birthdays, holidays)	

Can I afford what I'm saving up for?	

Money Left Over This Week	

(This is the **Total Amount Left** from your **Weekly Summary**, minus the **Amount Deposited** into your Savings Account)

Weekly Income				
Date	No. of Hours	Employer & Description	Via Cash /Bank?	Amount Paid
			Total Income	

Weekly Summary

Total Income	
Total Expenses	
Total	
Money Left Over from Last Week	
Total Amount Left	

Specific Things I'm Saving Up For

Item Description	How Much it Costs	Have I Got it Yet?
		☐
		☐
		☐
		☐

Weekly Expenses				
Date	Item(s) Bought	Purchased Where?	Via Cash /Bank?	Cost
			Total Expenses	

What will I do with my money?

Can I put some money into a Savings Account?	Existing Balance	Amount Deposited	New Savings Balance

Any expenses coming up that I need to remember? (e.g. birthdays, holidays)	

Can I afford what I'm saving up for?	

Money Left Over This Week	

(This is the **Total Amount Left** from your **Weekly Summary**, minus the **Amount Deposited** into your Savings Account)

Weekly Income

Date	No. of Hours	Employer & Description	Via Cash /Bank?	Amount Paid
			Total Income	

Weekly Summary

Total Income	
Total Expenses	
Total	
Money Left Over from Last Week	
Total Amount Left	

Specific Things I'm Saving Up For

Item Description	How Much it Costs	Have I Got it Yet?
		☐
		☐
		☐
		☐

Weekly Expenses

Date	Item(s) Bought	Purchased Where?	Via Cash /Bank?	Cost
		Total Expenses		

What will I do with my money?

Can I put some money into a Savings Account?	Existing Balance	Amount Deposited	New Savings Balance

Any expenses coming up that I need to remember? (e.g. birthdays, holidays)	

Can I afford what I'm saving up for?	

Money Left Over This Week	

(This is the **Total Amount Left** from your **Weekly Summary**, minus the **Amount Deposited** into your Savings Account)

Weekly Income				
Date	No. of Hours	Employer & Description	Via Cash /Bank?	Amount Paid
			Total Income	

Weekly Summary

Total Income	
Total Expenses	
Total	
Money Left Over from Last Week	
Total Amount Left	

Specific Things I'm Saving Up For

Item Description	How Much it Costs	Have I Got it Yet?
		☐
		☐
		☐
		☐

Weekly Expenses				
Date	Item(s) Bought	Purchased Where?	Via Cash /Bank?	Cost
			Total Expenses	

What will I do with my money?

Can I put some money into a Savings Account?	Existing Balance	Amount Deposited	New Savings Balance

Any expenses coming up that I need to remember? (e.g. birthdays, holidays)	

Can I afford what I'm saving up for?	

Money Left Over This Week	

(This is the **Total Amount Left** from your **Weekly Summary**, minus the **Amount Deposited** into your Savings Account)

Weekly Income

Date	No. of Hours	Employer & Description	Via Cash /Bank?	Amount Paid
			Total Income	

Weekly Summary

Total Income	
Total Expenses	
Total	
Money Left Over from Last Week	
Total Amount Left	

Specific Things I'm Saving Up For

Item Description	How Much it Costs	Have I Got it Yet?
		☐
		☐
		☐
		☐

Weekly Expenses

Date	Item(s) Bought	Purchased Where?	Via Cash /Bank?	Cost
			Total Expenses	

What will I do with my money?

Can I put some money into a Savings Account?	Existing Balance	Amount Deposited	New Savings Balance

Any expenses coming up that I need to remember? (e.g. birthdays, holidays)	

Can I afford what I'm saving up for?	

Money Left Over This Week	

(This is the **Total Amount Left** from your **Weekly Summary**, minus the **Amount Deposited** into your Savings Account)

Weekly Income				
Date	No. of Hours	Employer & Description	Via Cash /Bank?	Amount Paid
			Total Income	

Weekly Summary

Total Income	
Total Expenses	
Total	
Money Left Over from Last Week	
Total Amount Left	

Specific Things I'm Saving Up For

Item Description	How Much it Costs	Have I Got it Yet?
		☐
		☐
		☐
		☐

Weekly Expenses

Date	Item(s) Bought	Purchased Where?	Via Cash /Bank?	Cost
		Total Expenses		

What will I do with my money?

Can I put some money into a Savings Account?	Existing Balance	Amount Deposited	New Savings Balance

Any expenses coming up that I need to remember? (e.g. birthdays, holidays)	

Can I afford what I'm saving up for?	

Money Left Over This Week	

(This is the **Total Amount Left** from your **Weekly Summary**, minus the **Amount Deposited** into your Savings Account)

Weekly Income				
Date	No. of Hours	Employer & Description	Via Cash /Bank?	Amount Paid
			Total Income	

Weekly Summary

Total Income	
Total Expenses	
Total	
Money Left Over from Last Week	
Total Amount Left	

Specific Things I'm Saving Up For

Item Description	How Much it Costs	Have I Got it Yet?
		☐
		☐
		☐
		☐

Weekly Expenses				
Date	Item(s) Bought	Purchased Where?	Via Cash /Bank?	Cost
			Total Expenses	

What will I do with my money?

Can I put some money into a Savings Account?	Existing Balance	Amount Deposited	New Savings Balance

Any expenses coming up that I need to remember? (e.g. birthdays, holidays)	

Can I afford what I'm saving up for?	

Money Left Over This Week	

(This is the **Total Amount Left** from your **Weekly Summary**, minus the **Amount Deposited** into your Savings Account)

Weekly Income				
Date	No. of Hours	Employer & Description	Via Cash /Bank?	Amount Paid
			Total Income	

Weekly Summary

Total Income	
Total Expenses	
Total	
Money Left Over from Last Week	
Total Amount Left	

Specific Things I'm Saving Up For

Item Description	How Much it Costs	Have I Got it Yet?
		☐
		☐
		☐
		☐

Weekly Expenses

Date	Item(s) Bought	Purchased Where?	Via Cash /Bank?	Cost
		Total Expenses		

What will I do with my money?

Can I put some money into a Savings Account?	Existing Balance	Amount Deposited	New Savings Balance

Any expenses coming up that I need to remember? (e.g. birthdays, holidays)	

Can I afford what I'm saving up for?	

Money Left Over This Week	

(This is the **Total Amount Left** from your **Weekly Summary**, minus the **Amount Deposited** into your Savings Account)

Weekly Income

Date	No. of Hours	Employer & Description	Via Cash /Bank?	Amount Paid
			Total Income	

Weekly Summary

Total Income	
Total Expenses	
Total	
Money Left Over from Last Week	
Total Amount Left	

Specific Things I'm Saving Up For

Item Description	How Much it Costs	Have I Got it Yet?
		☐
		☐
		☐
		☐

Weekly Expenses				
Date	Item(s) Bought	Purchased Where?	Via Cash /Bank?	Cost
			Total Expenses	

What will I do with my money?

Can I put some money into a Savings Account?	Existing Balance	Amount Deposited	New Savings Balance

Any expenses coming up that I need to remember? (e.g. birthdays, holidays)	

Can I afford what I'm saving up for?	

Money Left Over This Week	

(This is the **Total Amount Left** from your **Weekly Summary**, minus the **Amount Deposited** into your Savings Account)

Weekly Income				
Date	No. of Hours	Employer & Description	Via Cash /Bank?	Amount Paid
			Total Income	

Weekly Summary

Total Income	
Total Expenses	
Total	
Money Left Over from Last Week	
Total Amount Left	

Specific Things I'm Saving Up For

Item Description	How Much it Costs	Have I Got it Yet?
		☐
		☐
		☐
		☐

Weekly Expenses

Date	Item(s) Bought	Purchased Where?	Via Cash /Bank?	Cost
		Total Expenses		

What will I do with my money?

Can I put some money into a Savings Account?	Existing Balance	Amount Deposited	New Savings Balance

Any expenses coming up that I need to remember? (e.g. birthdays, holidays)	

Can I afford what I'm saving up for?	

Money Left Over This Week	

(This is the **Total Amount Left** from your **Weekly Summary**, minus the **Amount Deposited** into your Savings Account)

Weekly Income

Date	No. of Hours	Employer & Description	Via Cash /Bank?	Amount Paid
			Total Income	

Weekly Summary

Total Income	
Total Expenses	
Total	
Money Left Over from Last Week	
Total Amount Left	

Specific Things I'm Saving Up For

Item Description	How Much it Costs	Have I Got it Yet?
		☐
		☐
		☐
		☐

Weekly Expenses

Date	Item(s) Bought	Purchased Where?	Via Cash /Bank?	Cost
			Total Expenses	

What will I do with my money?

Can I put some money into a Savings Account?	Existing Balance	Amount Deposited	New Savings Balance

Any expenses coming up that I need to remember? (e.g. birthdays, holidays)	

Can I afford what I'm saving up for?	

Money Left Over This Week	

(This is the **Total Amount Left** from your **Weekly Summary**, minus the **Amount Deposited** into your Savings Account)

Weekly Income

Date	No. of Hours	Employer & Description	Via Cash /Bank?	Amount Paid
			Total Income	

Weekly Summary

Total Income	
Total Expenses	
Total	
Money Left Over from Last Week	
Total Amount Left	

Specific Things I'm Saving Up For

Item Description	How Much it Costs	Have I Got it Yet?
		☐
		☐
		☐
		☐

Weekly Expenses

Date	Item(s) Bought	Purchased Where?	Via Cash /Bank?	Cost
			Total Expenses	

What will I do with my money?

Can I put some money into a Savings Account?	Existing Balance	Amount Deposited	New Savings Balance

Any expenses coming up that I need to remember? (e.g. birthdays, holidays)	

Can I afford what I'm saving up for?	

Money Left Over This Week	

(This is the **Total Amount Left** from your **Weekly Summary**, minus the **Amount Deposited** into your Savings Account)

Weekly Income

Date	No. of Hours	Employer & Description	Via Cash /Bank?	Amount Paid
			Total Income	

Weekly Summary

Total Income	
Total Expenses	
Total	
Money Left Over from Last Week	
Total Amount Left	

Specific Things I'm Saving Up For

Item Description	How Much it Costs	Have I Got it Yet?
		☐
		☐
		☐
		☐

\multicolumn{5}{c}{Weekly Expenses}
Date	Item(s) Bought	Purchased Where?	Via Cash /Bank?	Cost
			Total Expenses	

What will I do with my money?

Can I put some money into a Savings Account?	Existing Balance	Amount Deposited	New Savings Balance

Any expenses coming up that I need to remember? (e.g. birthdays, holidays)	

Can I afford what I'm saving up for?	

Money Left Over This Week	

(This is the **Total Amount Left** from your **Weekly Summary**, minus the **Amount Deposited** into your Savings Account)

Weekly Income

Date	No. of Hours	Employer & Description	Via Cash /Bank?	Amount Paid
			Total Income	

Weekly Summary

Total Income	
Total Expenses	
Total	
Money Left Over from Last Week	
Total Amount Left	

Specific Things I'm Saving Up For

Item Description	How Much it Costs	Have I Got it Yet?
		☐
		☐
		☐
		☐

Weekly Expenses				
Date	Item(s) Bought	Purchased Where?	Via Cash /Bank?	Cost
			Total Expenses	

What will I do with my money?

Can I put some money into a Savings Account?	Existing Balance	Amount Deposited	New Savings Balance

Any expenses coming up that I need to remember? (e.g. birthdays, holidays)	

Can I afford what I'm saving up for?	

Money Left Over This Week	

(This is the **Total Amount Left** from your **Weekly Summary**, minus the **Amount Deposited** into your Savings Account)

Weekly Income

Date	No. of Hours	Employer & Description	Via Cash /Bank?	Amount Paid
			Total Income	

Weekly Summary

Total Income	
Total Expenses	
Total	
Money Left Over from Last Week	
Total Amount Left	

Specific Things I'm Saving Up For

Item Description	How Much it Costs	Have I Got it Yet?
		☐
		☐
		☐
		☐

Weekly Expenses

Date	Item(s) Bought	Purchased Where?	Via Cash /Bank?	Cost
			Total Expenses	

What will I do with my money?

Can I put some money into a Savings Account?	Existing Balance	Amount Deposited	New Savings Balance

Any expenses coming up that I need to remember? (e.g. birthdays, holidays)	

Can I afford what I'm saving up for?	

Money Left Over This Week	

(This is the **Total Amount Left** from your **Weekly Summary**, minus the **Amount Deposited** into your Savings Account)

Weekly Income

Date	No. of Hours	Employer & Description	Via Cash /Bank?	Amount Paid
			Total Income	

Weekly Summary

Total Income	
Total Expenses	
Total	
Money Left Over from Last Week	
Total Amount Left	

Specific Things I'm Saving Up For

Item Description	How Much it Costs	Have I Got it Yet?
		☐
		☐
		☐
		☐

Weekly Expenses

Date	Item(s) Bought	Purchased Where?	Via Cash /Bank?	Cost
		Total Expenses		

What will I do with my money?

Can I put some money into a Savings Account?	Existing Balance	Amount Deposited	New Savings Balance

Any expenses coming up that I need to remember? (e.g. birthdays, holidays)	

Can I afford what I'm saving up for?	

Money Left Over This Week	

(This is the **Total Amount Left** from your **Weekly Summary**, minus the
Amount Deposited into your Savings Account)

Weekly Income

Date	No. of Hours	Employer & Description	Via Cash /Bank?	Amount Paid
			Total Income	

Weekly Summary

Total Income	
Total Expenses	
Total	
Money Left Over from Last Week	
Total Amount Left	

Specific Things I'm Saving Up For

Item Description	How Much it Costs	Have I Got it Yet?
		☐
		☐
		☐
		☐

Weekly Expenses

Date	Item(s) Bought	Purchased Where?	Via Cash /Bank?	Cost
		Total Expenses		

What will I do with my money?

Can I put some money into a Savings Account?	Existing Balance	Amount Deposited	New Savings Balance

Any expenses coming up that I need to remember? (e.g. birthdays, holidays)	

Can I afford what I'm saving up for?	

Money Left Over This Week	

(This is the **Total Amount Left** from your **Weekly Summary**, minus the **Amount Deposited** into your Savings Account)

Weekly Income				
Date	No. of Hours	Employer & Description	Via Cash /Bank?	Amount Paid
			Total Income	

Weekly Summary

Total Income	
Total Expenses	
Total	
Money Left Over from Last Week	
Total Amount Left	

Specific Things I'm Saving Up For

Item Description	How Much it Costs	Have I Got it Yet?
		☐
		☐
		☐
		☐

Weekly Expenses

Date	Item(s) Bought	Purchased Where?	Via Cash /Bank?	Cost
			Total Expenses	

What will I do with my money?

Can I put some money into a Savings Account?	Existing Balance	Amount Deposited	New Savings Balance

Any expenses coming up that I need to remember? (e.g. birthdays, holidays)	

Can I afford what I'm saving up for?	

Money Left Over This Week	

(This is the **Total Amount Left** from your **Weekly Summary**, minus the **Amount Deposited** into your Savings Account)

Weekly Income

Date	No. of Hours	Employer & Description	Via Cash /Bank?	Amount Paid
			Total Income	

Weekly Summary

Total Income	
Total Expenses	
Total	
Money Left Over from Last Week	
Total Amount Left	

Specific Things I'm Saving Up For

Item Description	How Much it Costs	Have I Got it Yet?
		☐
		☐
		☐
		☐

Weekly Expenses

Date	Item(s) Bought	Purchased Where?	Via Cash /Bank?	Cost
		Total Expenses		

What will I do with my money?

Can I put some money into a Savings Account?	Existing Balance	Amount Deposited	New Savings Balance

Any expenses coming up that I need to remember? (e.g. birthdays, holidays)	

Can I afford what I'm saving up for?	

Money Left Over This Week	

(This is the **Total Amount Left** from your **Weekly Summary**, minus the **Amount Deposited** into your Savings Account)

Weekly Income

Date	No. of Hours	Employer & Description	Via Cash /Bank?	Amount Paid
			Total Income	

Weekly Summary

Total Income	
Total Expenses	
Total	
Money Left Over from Last Week	
Total Amount Left	

Specific Things I'm Saving Up For

Item Description	How Much it Costs	Have I Got it Yet?
		☐
		☐
		☐
		☐

Weekly Expenses				
Date	Item(s) Bought	Purchased Where?	Via Cash /Bank?	Cost
			Total Expenses	

What will I do with my money?

Can I put some money into a Savings Account?	Existing Balance	Amount Deposited	New Savings Balance

Any expenses coming up that I need to remember? (e.g. birthdays, holidays)	

Can I afford what I'm saving up for?	

Money Left Over This Week	

(This is the **Total Amount Left** from your **Weekly Summary**, minus the **Amount Deposited** into your Savings Account)

Made in the USA
Coppell, TX
27 November 2019